Breath of the Onion

Italian-American Anecdotes

Books by Franco Pagnucci
  Tracks on Damp Sand (North Star Press, 2014)
  All That Is Left (Chapbook, Red Ochre Lit, 2012)
  Ancient Moves (Bur Oak Press, 1998)
  I Never Had a Pet (Bur Oak Press, 1992)
  Out Harmsen's Way (Fireweed Press, 1991)

Anthologies Edited by Franco Pagnucci
  New Roads Old Towns (A Rountree Publication, UW-Platteville, 1988)
  Face the Poem (Bur Oak Press, 1979)

Breath of the Onion

Italian-American Anecdotes

Franco Pagnucci

for Iole Francioni (1915-2012)

Cover art, *North of Town*, copyright © Anna Pagnucci

Copyright © 2015 Franco Pagnucci

ISBN 978-87839-791-4

First Edition: March 2015

Printed in the United States of America.

Published by
North Star Press of St. Cloud, Inc.
P.O. Box 451
St. Cloud, Minnesota 56302

northstarpress.com

Contents

One: I Won't See You Again

Two: A Shortcut to Altopascio

Three: In America

One:

I Won't See You Again

Taste for Fruit

I could say it's from my father. There's the story of the homesick soldier in Genoa at dawn. Fabio from the mountain village of Ruota climbs a tree he had seen the day before in a stranger's garden. The grapefruit tree is loaded with yellowy-bright fruit, and Fabio climbs to pick and fill his pockets with the biggest, largest oranges he's imagined and can reach. Hurrying, before sunrise, he peels one and bites in. It's not the mouth-watering, sweet juice, but a sour, bitter taste he doesn't know.

The blind man's vineyard on the upper side of the rocky path that climbed the hill at the back of the Church of St. Bartholomew was protected by a high wall of mortared stones. The top of the wall was rounded and embedded with shards of glass. The wall whispered a forbidden place.

But the grapes. You could see the golden hanging orbs if you stood on tip-toes, on the bank along the opposite side of the path. Those juicy muscatel grapes on the sunny side of the hill looked plump and ready.

Those hanging grapes. You looked at them every time you passed—they were so huge. At night you went to sleep tasting their sweetness.

Who hasn't dreamt of sneaking into an orchard along a river, below a private girls' school or into a strawberry patch in the garden above the school, where on late afternoons the girls waved at you from the high dorm windows above and beyond—the girls with long hair blowing in the wind coming in the windows?

I scaled that glass-embedded wall into the blind man's vineyard and ate grapes like an eye-crazed bird, but out of nowhere the all-knowing blind man rushed out, scolding, his walking staff raised high over his head, the white eyes glaring . . . I ran and leapt at the wall like a trapped rabbit.

Next day, hot red welts were on me and a fever. I stayed in bed. Afraid to go back to sleep, I kept the covers over my head.

Only later, maybe months later, Aunt Maria *Nuova* coaxed me by the hand, under the windows of his house and past. We were headed for a drink from the mountain spring to quench a summer's thirst.

I don't remember if I ever felt sorry for my act. You know how ripe fruit can dazzle any of us. I remember looking up and telling Aunt Maria how the blind man had scared me half to death. "I hope he dies," I said. Not long after that the old blind man died.

I think his death was really not my doing, but then I think how every bird's wing-beat moves the air it touches, and I think how every wave of air must shift, a little, something else.

The Door

How the wind whirled and whined under the gap of that door, and every gust beating at the house whapped that door against its hinges.

Papà and uncles were gone. Only old grandfathers were around and a few young men who hid when the Nazi raiders came. But cabbage and bean soup steamed on the stove, and *Nonno* and I sat at the kitchen table.

The mountain, *La Cima*, sometimes was capped with snow. Once it caught a C-47 on its peak.

Nonna's (*Inzuppa*) Cabbage and Bean Soup Recipe

¾ cup dried Cannellini beans (white beans, kidney beans), soaked overnight in water and drained
¼ cup extra-virgin olive oil
2 Spanish or red onions, cut into ½ inch chunks
2 leeks, white and light-green parts, sliced thinly and rinsed
2 carrots cut into ¼ inch dice
2 ribs celery cut into ¼ inch slices
2 medium red potatoes cut into ½ inch slices
2 cloves garlic sliced thinly
2 sprigs thyme
2 sprigs rosemary
1 bay leaf
1 lb. black cabbage (Tuscan kale or other kale), roughly chopped
½ lb. green cabbage roughly chopped
Salt and freshly ground pepper, to taste
2 T tomato paste

1. Put Cannellini beans in 4 qt. pan, and cover with 2 inches water. Bring to a boil, and simmer about 45 min.
2. While beans are cooking, heat oil in 8 qt. pan until hot but not smoking. Add onions, leeks, carrots, celery, potatoes, garlic, and herbs, and cook until vegetables begin to soften, about 5 min. Add kale and cabbage, and cook until these wilt and soften, about 10 min.
3. Drain beans and add to vegetables. Add cool water to cover by 2 inches. Bring to a boil, then simmer for 45 min.
4. *Nonna* would put chunks of heavy, old, dry, crusty bread in a bowl and ladle soup over the chunks. The soup would soften the bread (thus the Italian *Inzuppa*—moistened bread soup). We sometimes serve chunks of heavy bread to dunk into the soup, and we often grate Parmesan or Asiago cheese over the soup.

Even the thought of cabbage and bean soup is a warm, happy comfort now. Though the world might be blowing away, I remember the warmth and security of *Nonna's* kitchen.

Sunday Hat

In the wine cellar, I'd be standing at Grandfather's side, and he, still wearing his Sunday hat, now knelt on one knee and filled the lunch bottle from the barrel with the wooden spigot. He would tilt his head away from me. "Don't you . . . Don't you touch Christ's hat," he'd say, as the fragrant dark wine poured with an echo into the bottle and he waited for me to push his hat off again.

We'd laugh those Sunday mornings, and he carried me up the stairs, piggy-back and holding on like a rider, his breaths full of wheezing.

In the steamy kitchen, *Nonna*, standing at the table, served cabbage and bean soup over our plates of chunks of hard bread, *Nonno Favilla's* at the head of the table, mine close on its right.

Butchering Time

The squeals of the pigs haunted fall nights when I was young.

Once when I opened *Nonno Cecco's* barn door a crack, I saw the pig on the dirt floor, on his back, pinned down between two men's arms and knees. The third man, Uncle Ivo, knelt on one knee and, leaning over the pig, shoved the sharpened spike in—below the pink mound of belly and raised left leg—and held the steel shaft in with all his weight against it.

Blood spurted, and I heard the squeal, and then more squeals filled the barn to the rafters. I closed the door and stood before it in the dark.

Fall dusks fell sooner, as well as the chill air. Playtime was shorter. School. School again and *Papà's* stern whistle on the wind came too soon and the fear of his raised thin belt. Over the town, the shrill squeals of other pigs were unmistakable.

Later, in America, when I visited and slept at an unfamiliar aunt's in Chicago and I awoke in the night, far, far from home, and heard the wail of a siren across the darkness, I shivered and felt a dread rise for some other, some creature's struggle in the dark. The feeling of homesickness which filled me then, so many years ago, and even now is so familiar must be our kin, preparing us for the shivers and dread of a soul stepping out from the warmth of the flesh.

After the War

Upstairs in the mill where the flour grinders were, *Papà* made us eggs from the chickens that pecked in the yard, while below us the first olives churned under huge stone wheels that rolled and rolled over them in those stone tubs and made them ooze their green.

The scrambled eggs, runny with new oil, would be a thick green you had forgotten, and the fragrance of hot olive oil filled the upper mill to the high rafters. I'd come into that smell with a pocketful of small, cold November apples, red-flecked and crisp and tangy. Our fathers were back from the War. What more could you want on a fall afternoon?

Grandfather Francesco's Kitchen

The flicker flew and flapped his wings against the top of the window screen and slid down, claws scratching, wings beating. He flew up the other side and flapped, flapped and clawed, scratching and sliding down—his bill, poking and poking.

Papà had snatched this woodpecker with yellow-lined wings out of a hollow stump of a chestnut tree in *Nonno Cecco's* old timbered hillside above Catevetto. He'd gunny-sacked him, and let him loose in Grandfather's old kitchen.

From the window the bird flew around the dim lit ceiling of the kitchen and even went into the dark parlor, searching . . . then came back . . .

In America, *Mamma* said, years later, her ten years in that kitchen of *Nonno Cecco's* house were like a prison sentence.

. . . That bird came back—black bill like the tip of an arrow, fiery red crescent on the nape, guiding the arrow—and slammed against the bottom of the screen and ripped free and up, up above the narrow street and tall houses, up into the cold blue dusk.

Come December

I'd be on the lookout in hills and ravines for the shiny, greenest mosses and anxious until *Papà* relented and set up in the front corner of the parlor, two sawhorses with boards across them and on top of the boards, two benches, one on each side, for hills. Then, *Mamma* would spread old sheets over these, and I would begin carefully laying the mosses I'd gathered and stored in a dampened burlap bag.

Early Christmas Eve the parish priest appeared. You never knew the exact time or what the awards would be. This year *Papà* had promised a light in the star, only it shorted when we switched it on, as the priest came in and straightened the white surplus he was wearing . . . *Papà* had ducked behind the hills of moss and birch branches we'd fastened along the back of the boards, for trees, and he held the two wires in place.

In the dark parlor, the starlight speckled the birch leaves onto the ceiling with a mysterious splendor and over the shepherds on the mossy hills and over us, awaiting the child.

Half a Fried Egg

"Come, come look!" *Papà's* mother, *Nonna* Carola, a tiny, five-foot-two woman, said, motioning me to the rectory's kitchen window where she'd been standing and half-smiling as she looked out at Egisto, Uncle Jerry, her six-foot son from America. Split logs arced off his axe, off the splitting-stump. "Have you ever seen such . . . power . . . and . . . What strength!" she said.

She was at the stove as Uncle Jerry came in with a waft of sweat and pine dust. She had fried him five eggs from the two dozen he'd bought that morning, and she served him, before splitting one between her plate and mine.

"Half an egg?" he said.

"Half an egg is plenty for a child," *Nonna* said. "With two slices of bread, it will—"

"Half an egg!" he said. "Go on." He tried to reach toward the table and the paper sack he'd brought, but *Nonna* deflected his hand. "I'll throw the whole bunch . . ." He pointed to the edge of the garden where he'd been splitting wood.

"I'm not sure how that scene ended, but I can still taste the half-egg and crusty bread *Nonna* Carola gave me," I said on the phone to Cousin Esterina, who lives in Niles, outside Chicago.

She laughed. "Uncle Egisto was good show-off. He bring big American car to Italy."

"Probably a Buick Park Avenue," I said.

"I do fifth grade, living with *Nonna* Carola at Uncle Remo's rectory. *Nonna* Carola was tough, hard grandma. I didn't like *Nonna* Carola," Cousin Esterina said. "*Nonno Cecco*, I love."

Idle Hands

To be home by dark, *Papà* would have left early, the echoes of Moro's hooves and the Sunday trap hard to remember.

Then the sun would be behind the mountains, dark valleys below, and across on the far sky, a warm orange, turning pink, cooling toward violet, then blue, then dark.

Suddenly I would feel the falling dark pressing down, the endless summer looming, and the night heavy around my bed on the parlor couch.

You have to imagine long idle days for a boy spending the summer with a severe grandmother and in the confines of an uncle priest's rectory, walled garden, and churchyard in the mountains with falling away valleys of vineyards.

Nonna Carola had come on a mission—her youngest, a priest, and, at twenty-seven, in his own first parish in the rich wine country of San Pietro a Marcigliano. The young housekeeper, although a cousin, was sent home. *Nonna* Carola didn't want people to talk. *Mamma's* brother would later say with a chuckle, "Maria was sent back home because she was full of life." He'd hold his hands out, palms up, to show what he meant—the large size of her breasts.

And I saw women old and young stop by the rectory Sunday mornings after Mass. They left baskets—breads, cheeses, wine, figs, and jams for Uncle.

He was soft spoken, a listener and a gentle man. He fixed clocks, and he had a shiny black piano that he played and a black automobile he kept polished and fine-tuned. He would give you a lift if you needed one. That summer he taught me how to serve at Mass and how to eat with a knife and fork.

If with a bamboo spear I killed a prowling cat in his walled-in garden, it's no reflection on Uncle Priest. *Mamma* always said, "Idle hands are the devil's workshop."

Nonno Cecco

He is sitting in a chair at the back and facing the window as he usually does in the warmth of the afternoon sun, only now he has asked to see me. I have come, and he is handing me the Elgin pocket watch Uncle Jerry had sent him, after seventeen years—a peace gesture.

"I won't see you again," *Nonno Cecco* is saying. "America is far away. Far. Far." The whites of his eyes have redness along the rims.

We're in the new kitchen of Grandfather's house. This kitchen was added when Uncle Ivo and Aunt Albertina married and moved into *Nonno Cecco's* house. Uncle Ivo and Aunt Albertina are not there. Uncle had words with my father over the bedroom set my father thought was his and sold because we're going to America.

Iole and the Crèche Statuettes

Aunt Iole insisted—she'd walked me home. She would go into *Nonno Cecco's* house with or without me. She'd talk to *Papà* about making room in the trunk. "*Papà* will have to hit me first," she said. "He won't hit you again." She took my hand and pulled me in behind her.

Papà's face was sweaty. I went to the dark back corner of the parlor. My heart pounded. Aunt Iole seemed so short and thin, standing, facing my father. In my mind, now, she sailed us in like a yawl, sails full-wind to confront this man who was my father. She could well have been King Eurytus's daughter, the Greek princess loved by Heracles. Those days, when my father set his mind, it would have taken such a woman to change him.

It was edging toward midnight on that late April when *Mamma* and *Papà* packed our trunk. In the end I got to bring my whole set of crèche statuettes, but later, in America, I found that the plaster of Paris had softened and the paint had mostly flaked off.

Il Gatto

Vitolino, Violetta's son, was short and wiry. We called him *Gatto* because of his moves and because he was tough, like a tomcat. He was daring, too, and an expert bird trapper. He could climb a fruit tree and scoot along a branch out, out, like a bud-feeding partridge, even as the branch bent and bobbed underneath him. There, he would tie the sticky tar-coated sticks like an extra perch for birds to get stuck onto.

But *Gatto* was at his best with stones and the way he could set the heaviest traps. With a thin stick he would prop a heavy flagstone, in silty dirt, on edge and lean it, one side onto the thin stick. The bottom of this thin stick would sit on a wafer chip of stone that sat on a pebble for a pivot. He would cover the wafer chip with the fine silt and sprinkle a few bread crumbs on top.

Imagine the sudden surprise for the bird that stepped on the chip or pecked at the crumbs on that dust-covered wafer—the heavy flagstone would come down like a slap and kill that bird, but without smashing it. That was the best trick.

I don't remember why I was surprised and caught that day by one of *Gatto's* stones.

It was the day before *Papà*, *Mamma*, little brother, and I were leaving for America. Michele and I had climbed the wall above the ravine, and we stood in the road below the rectory of the twelfth century Church of St. Bartholomew, the apostle about whom Jesus was to have said, "here is a man in whom there is no deception," the apostle who was flayed and then crucified. The church was up the hill road and at the back of the rectory.

I had turned to look behind me for *Gatto*, who was a head shorter than we were. He'd been complaining about our pace up the side of the ravine and falling farther behind, and I saw how he had just gotten to the wall and must have stopped. I saw, at that moment, the top of his cap, his forehead, and then his eyes clear the rim of the wall and look at me.

And as sudden, I saw the flick of his arm arcing over the wall, and I saw the flat, jagged-edged dust-colored stone fly out of his hand and felt a glancing thud and sting on my left brow, and I felt warm liquid run over my closed eyelid to my cheek, and I saw Vitolino *Gatto* come over the wall like a cat and run up the road toward the town.

"Let's see, let's see. Let me see," Michele was saying. "You're bleeding. There's blood from your eye down your cheek," he said.

It wasn't my eye. It was my left brow that puffed and crusted with blood in the cut, as early next morning I was in the street looking and calling, "*Gatto! Gatto!*" but we were leaving. *Nonno Favilla* was waiting for me as I walked up to the courtyard.

"*Va bene,*"—it's okay, he said. "You're going to America and Vitolino has to stay. That's why he threw the stone. You're going to America," *Nonno Favilla* said. "Your brow will heal over, and you'll forget the pain. It will be fine for you in America." His eyes reddened along the edges.

He Stands In the Courtyard

Until I thought about him, I never missed him or missed how easily everything's gone.

Nonno Favilla, Mamma's father, the pushover, stands in the courtyard even as I think. He leans down for a kiss and to say he can't stay to watch us leave. I know his wheezing, the coarse mustache, and the warmth already coming up out of his vest and jacket and shirtfront, this early April dawn.

He stands in the courtyard where Michele and *Gatto* and I had played marbles and sometimes the same game with walnuts. *Nonno* stands as he stood that morning on the hard dirt of the courtyard, and then he walks back toward the house. Everyone else has come out now: *Nonna Nunziata*, Aunt Iole, New Aunt Maria, Old Aunt Maria, Uncle Gino, and the neighbors Landina and her husband Endro. My friend Michele, Landina and Endro's son, probably was looking down from his window, though I don't remember seeing him when I looked up.

In the flurry of leaving I forget *Nonno Favilla*, though, now, I hear him walking back out to the courtyard after the rest have gone back in. *Nonno* is standing alone on the packed dirt of the courtyard, listening.

Two:

A Shortcut to Altopascio

Landina's World

The woman in a black dress we find in the church cemetery is Landina, *Mamma's* best friend from their girlhood, and she says she is there for her husband and shows us. *"Sì,"* yes, I say, speaking Italian. "I remember big Andrew." I raise my right hand to indicate.

He had gotten rich in America and gone back to Italy to live and marry.

"He wasn't so big or as wealthy as people made out," she says. "He was a good man. Hard worker, though that didn't save him either."

She shows my wife and me around, and as we walk, we pause so Landina can point to the tombs. She calls out the names and makes connections between our two families, among the dead ones. With a hand raised palm down above her right knee, she shows how tall I was the last time she saw me. I called her, *"Zia,"*—Aunt, she says, and was like her own son, Michele, who is a grocer in Pisa, now, and with two young children. Do I remember his curls like mine? "He, too, has lost most of his hair. What's to be done?" Landina says. "We get old. The town is full of aged widows."

I nod and smile.

Even this cemetery at the back of St. Bartholomew's Church is smaller than I remember. In an instant, we've walked around it.

Landina is seventy-nine. Her hair is mostly dark, dark gray. At dawn she's in her garden, the best kept plot in the village.

The Bed

A beamed low ceiling slanted just above the half-sized window that gave the room a blink of light.

The bed wasn't *Nonna* and *Nonno Favilla's*. Visiting American relatives had replaced it, and others had slept, soundly, no doubt, in the new bed. My wife and I awoke in the night. We were out of breath.

Rabbit Hutch

Imagine my look and you photographing my head in the
second story window of this reminder of *Papà's* inheritance—
the rabbit hutch *Nonno Cecco* and Uncle Ivo had mortared out
of red clay bricks they had made.

I must have remembered with a blush. The panes were gone
and the floor on which one spring a younger cousin and I ex-
plored our parts, above the nibbling rabbits.

Losses and Saviors
for *Nonna Nunziata* (from *Annunziata*—"Annunciation")

I.

"Here," Aunt Iole said, coming back with a faded rosy-colored box. "You asked me to keep these for you. That you'd come back to get them."

I had forgotten. It had been forty years. I opened the small, square box which this unmarried sister of *Mamma's* had kept all these years—this aunt who had mostly raised me when *Papà* was gone to the War and *Mamma*, newly married, had moved into *Nonno Cecco's* house, across the piazza and up the north hill part of the town. I picked up the small pocket knife with its sides of shiny red and green miniature tiles, a few missing, and set it down. I gently nudged the large marble shooter with the white lightning streaks, ran the nail of my index finger along the edge of the yellow flicker feather, looked at the green and the black fountain pens, and looked at the terra cotta festival whistle shaped like an uncircumcised child's penis. "Isn't this something?" I said to my wife, extending the box toward her, across the small parlor table. "I remember the pocket knife," I said.

She declined with a nod, and the sad look of her blue eyes made me understand I shouldn't take anything. I wish I had realized, then, that after the War when we left, I had left forever and that all the little things from that childhood of forty years ago belonged to Aunt Iole.

II.

Even now I taste the small loss as Aunt Iole, too, would remember it among those extractions that leave crackles on the heart. I wish I hadn't taken the fountain pens, even for a symbol.

But here I am, *Nonna*. I've come to lie in your bed, again, as on that first night after you'd announced that I was too old now to sleep with Aunt Iole in her bed. So I'll lie, here, while you and *Nonno Favilla* exchange prayer parts, making an arch of them over me. I am sleepy and warm, and my feet warm up, even without the hot brick Aunt and I usually needed.

III.

Really, this has to be for Aunt Iole, more, for she had faced down my father that night of the packing. Aunt Iole, who knew I was leaving for a far away America and who would have taken my father's blow for me, Aunt Iole, who that night had saved my dream for my crèche statuettes in the new land. It was that Aunt Iole, who for forty years had kept for my return a small box with the few other things I had treasured.

Violetta's Door

Waiting for a breath of cool evening air, she sat on a wooden kitchen chair against the outside wall of her house, on the narrow street, fronting her door. The door framed a black interior where the day's heat would be choking dark rooms above the steep stairs and narrow cellar.

I remember her and her son, I insist, touching the scar on my left brow.

"Long time ago," she says. "He never meant the stone . . ." she points part way up toward my brow, and then lets her hand drop to her lap. "That one . . . He died."

"The Cancer. Years ago," she says, after a bit.

I remember warm blood in my eye. *Nonno Favilla* upset. In the morning leaving for America. I remember up the dark stairs, the hot, dark kitchen, Violetta sitting on a chair in a corner, her huge, naked breasts, drooping to her lap. She nursed a child, as her son Vitolino, "*Gatto*"—The Cat—and I ran through, playing.

Water and Words Before Sunrise

On this second year of drought and another hot, dry July, the small concrete pool gathers the trickle of water coming down from the mountain to Landina's garden—the upper plot before the trees run up the mountainside.

You have to imagine the neighbor, a gardener hardly middle-aged, tall and blond and blue-eyed and with an Irish tongue, turning Italian, in a twelfth-century Tuscan village.

The small pool owner, at seventy-nine, compact as a green onion and still in a black dress, though her husband's been dead for three years, is saying, "Nora, you can't leave the hose running, as I've said before." She speaks from her bean rows, without turning, without looking down at the terraced strips in the garden plot below hers, and all the while, she is scratching at one of her thighs with the tip of the hand sickle.

Nora hoes with her back bent in half, her backside toward Landina.

"Hoeing like that is a sure pain in the back," Landina says. "I've said that too often to the wrong end."

Nora is married to one of *Papà's* cousins on his mother's side, an Italian-American who came back to live on the home place after retirement but is back in the States at this time. Nora will say, later, "Landina, a cup of *Orzo*? Come down in a minute, Landina. Give your heart a rest."

In America, before her marriage, Nora was a nurse, though in Ruota no one trusts her funny-sounding Italian words.

"I'll boil the water," she'll say to Landina, who will come with her hands washed and with her crocheting to have a cup of Nestle's *Orzo* on Nora's shaded veranda.

Cousin Rosalba, "Rose of Dawn"

From afar I saw Rosalba, sprinkling herbs over the kitchen landscape, and had to stop. Some she sifted out of her hand as if she was sowing seeds clockwise from the outside, in narrowing circles to the center of the great pan's sauce and meat mixture. Some herbs she tossed from above—a sharp accent let go—allowing the thyme leaves to speak and fall where they wanted.

Aunt Iole pointed to the large platter of flan in which Rosalba had fanned peach slices into yellow petals around the center of the custard. And all the while she seasoned the bubbling mixture, she talked to you (though you didn't understand Italian) and thus, to me, as she talked to the herbs. It was as if she had us by the hand and for the feast she was leading us to the specific chair in which we'd feel the most comfortable—it fit us so, boosting our backs, framing our postures.

I see her almond face half-turned toward us in this frameable photo. Her husband must have been close by, catching in the photo how we saw her and how he felt in her presence. How she made us all feel.

Cousin Rosalba's Fried Zucchini and Zucchini Flowers Recipe

2 medium zucchini (10-12 inches)
12 zucchini flowers
2 eggs
1 cup flour
Canola oil for frying
Deep frying pan

1. Wash and cut zucchini into ¼-inch rounds. Heat about ½ inch of oil in pan. Beat eggs in a shallow dish and add fresh ground pepper. With fork tine spear zucchini rounds and dip in egg mixture, then in flour, then in egg mixture again. Fry them.
2. Wash zucchini flowers (making sure to check insides for bugs). Pat dry, and dip in egg mixture, then flour, then in egg mixture again. Fry along with zucchini rounds. While frying, both items usually float. As one side gets golden, turn over. Spread a couple paper towels on a large, flat dish. When both sides of zucchini and zucchini flowers are golden, lift out of pan with a slotted spatula, letting the oil drain away, and place the zucchini rounds and zucchini flowers on paper towels to drain away excess oils.

We sometimes serve this as a side dish with pulled pork or Sloppy Joe sandwiches.

A Shortcut to Altopascio

I'm driving the rental car. Uncle Ivo sits up front, my wife in the back, and in the dark we pass through Padule, where, as a child forty years before, I came from Ruota with *Papà* to make hay. A meadow on the left feels familiar even in darkness, and I remember the abandoned robin's nest with three aqua-blue eggs I found in the fallen tree along the canal.

We don't stop. It's late, and Uncle Ivo says, not a safe place anymore. At the stop sign, over the short bridge where the mountain road from Ruota turns left toward Altopascio, a woman a few years older than our middle-school daughter steps out of the darkness and toward our car and opens her black dress. When she notices a woman in the back seat, she rewraps her dress around her and spins on her stiletto heels laced up her calves like Roman sandals.

I drive on, airing the images in my memory, in this, the world they must travel.

A Poet In Rome

My cousin Gina helps me find the poet on a narrow uphill street in the center of the old city. Climbing the long dark stairs to her third-floor rooms, I imagine, at the touch of pen to paper, drawers full of cantos and piled scraps of paper with sly lines, swallows rising above the excavations . . .

"Too lazy," she says, "to have answered your letter . . . No, not too busy writing. Just lazy."

She has come out from the back to stand at her desk. She shakes three small white pills out of a green disk, swallows them, twists a long cigarette into a long brown holder, lights the cigarette with a shaky hand, then walks toward the middle of the room and lies down on her right side, her head toward the foot of the bed. She faces me for a photo—half smiling, tired and thin and too pale from being too much indoors. Her teeth need work.

I refocus the lens.

I think back to Wisconsin, my Iowa dentist for her. He has been to Vietnam. He'd like the authentic oldness of her quarters. He would be gentle.

I think of her lyrics, raved over before she was thirty. She hasn't published now for almost ten years.

She gets up and hands me two of her books, the cover of one stained with half a ring from a coffee cup. There are only two copies of each book in the apartment. "If you want the poems," she says, "you must make yourself copies." She lies back down on the bed in the same poetic position.

We chat.

She doesn't rise as we leave. Even her bare feet look too thin.

"That's a consumed woman," Gina, my Roman cousin, says as we go down the long dark stairs. I imagine Gina feeding the poet's poems, filling them with stuffed green peppers runny with olive oil. "And she's no Roman," my cousin says in the street. "Umbrian," she says. "There was no hospitality."

Driving Italy

In Florence, it was crazy, every car trying to justify itself.

"You need to go right," my wife said.

I was in the inside lane, rounding the hub again, a leaf on a spoke. Four cars in two lanes, plus motorcycles, vespas, and bikes in between. So maybe I blinked and headed right. Still, how did I manage it?

You had to maneuver semaphores the same way or wait for the hereafter.

From Rome, heading back to Tuscany, we went off the *Autostrada* and along the coast, for the sea, and once I got brave and tried the passing lane in the middle, but an oncoming car cut into that lane and sped toward me. I was there first—I had heard the rule—but I wasn't playing "chicken." I had nothing to prove. I swerved across the left lane and off the highway, to the grassy shoulder and waited . . . Wondered how many passed and laughed.

I waited for a breathing space without cars before going back across and into the right lane.

We never saw the sea.

From the Windows of the Uffizi Gallery

We wandered through the rooms and the names and the paintings—the *Madonnas* of Cimabue, Giotto, Masolino, and Masaccio. Paolo Uccello's *Battle of San Romano* with the dead gray horses down in front. Filippo Lippi's sweet, sensual *Madonna with Child*. The Duke of Urbino's face with moles and beard stubble. Botticelli's *Venus* coming out of the sea and to shore on an enormous shell. Leonardo's *Annunciation* with pine trees I recognized. Michelangelo's *Holy Family* so solid, so grounded, it gave one faith. Titian's naked Venus and a sleeping puppy on a white sheet and red couch—so warm you could embrace her.

You said I often stood with my mouth open, but it was stuffy and hot in the rooms that went on into farther and more rooms.

We drank water from our heavy bottles, and then could go on.

When we looked out from the third floor windows, below us the roofs of the Ponte Vecchio, the Old Bridge, went orange in the turning light and the Arno, a green, green—like the Chicago River always did on St. Patrick's Day—and I thought of Florence as containable, and with one hand, grafted it, neatly, corner to corner for you.

"Nothing is so simple," you said, looking out once more, and then heading for the street.

I followed you in the downpour and the exhaust fumes that now hung over the street like a heavy lid on a pot, and I wondered how the Florentine air was in Dante's day.

"Too bad beauty is only beauty from above," I said, thinking of the light and us standing in the rooms looking and standing at the windows looking down. But this, this was the world, and following all the rushing passers, we, too, rushed to the canopied goldsmiths' shops, lining both sides of the covered bridge, where the lights in the display windows full of gold made the air under the canopies and all the stopped-lookers golden.

"Do you want some of this?" I said, pointing to a necklace and earring loops. "How about—this? . . . This?" I pointed into windows as we walked in the glowing, golden heat.

"I only wanted to look," my wife said, pulling me away by the hand.

The Church of San Pietro a Marcigliano

Scaffolding of old boards holds up the archway to the church door, and the door is mortared-in with brick. Uncle Priest's bedroom with the shiny, black upright piano is air. Half the rectory is gone. Only the old man on a backless chair in front of the corner store, on the street below the churchyard, remembers anything.

"Everyone is gone or dead," he says. "The new marquis inherited the lands and lets them lie. Soon there'll be no one who'll know what to do. The vineyards are entangled in thorns." He spits the way *Nonno Cecco* did on the floor of his old kitchen. *Mamma* hated cleaning it up.

I climb the wall of the rectory cellar, where Uncle Priest kept the black car Uncle Jerry sent him money from America to buy. I look down into a pit of blackberry thorns.

Always the world we remember is blowing away, and every day we yearn to go back.

The Fish, the Wife, the Mother

The fish came from the festival in the church piazza in Altopascio. Still, Cousin Teresina had put two days' preparation on this dinner for her friend Nora and her young son and for Uncle Ivo and us, but Cousin Teresina's son said, "This cream cake is not your usual." He was twenty-two and shoved the dish with the square of desert to the side. "Taste it yourself," he said. "It's disgusting." She was standing behind him, and he never turned toward her but spoke over a shoulder.

Cousin Teresina picked the dish up off the table and stood behind him and tasted the cream cake and said, "Is it bad?" and tasted some more and said, "Is it that bad, really? I can't tell." And she ate it.

She hadn't sat at all. Through the dinner's many courses she carried platters and dishes in and out of the kitchen and, besides, rushed when her husband shouted, "Bread! More bread! *Vino! Vino! Vino ancora!*"

We guests had praised Cousin Teresina's dinner, and now we praised and praised her cream cake, and she thanked us, but nothing we said seemed to matter.

Macaroni In Castelvecchio

"May he rest in peace! He was my brother," Uncle Ivo said to Cousin Pia, "but I'd have taken his chamber pot after . . . and dumped it on his face." He spoke without a blink of his blue eyes.

"Uncle, what could I do?" Cousin Pia said. "He was my mother's husband. He was my father. The Parkinson's had diminished him. He couldn't lift a hand for himself anymore." She was setting the table. "Nothing fancy," she said.

Her napkins were linen.

"No one could have done more for him. Still, he never accepted you, never treated you like a daughter," Uncle said. "And he left you nothing. What kind of skin was he?"

"Uncle, to me he was my father," Cousin Pia said, her brown eyes and barley-colored skin tired-looking but with a softness of a pasta *fresca*.

We sat down, and she brought the fresh *sagnarelli* (macaroni), thin, silk-smooth rectangular strips two inches long, with fluted edges. She had made them early that dawn of *durum semolina* flour the color of her skin.

Through the rabbit stew and roast chicken and stuffed peppers, the blue cheese and peaches, the apple cake and the coffee, Uncle went on, at times punctuating the air with his knife and fork, whichever utensil and hand were uppermost at the moment. It was the principle he was arguing, and for our benefit, my wife's and mine especially. I knew since in his kitchen on those late nights he had said I should write things. So, here he was the supporting Uncle Ivo, arguing the principle of what was owed by his dead brother, Romolo, step-father he never legally became to this woman whose father was the older brother, Amato—Amato, who had died in Argentina. In Uncle Ivo's mind this was a piece of family-history and of injustice.

Cousin Pia's husband Vasco, a talker, was present too, and must have had things to say. I know he kept passing the wine and later exchanged some of our dollars for lire. "Better deal than at the bank," he said. But that's all I remember about him that night. He would never have missed what Uncle Ivo was doing, and Vasco would have decided to yield the floor for his wife's benefit.

Uncle Ivo did mention how fine Cousin Pia's macaroni strips were—"So thin and smooth," he said, "they slide down on their own."

The Horse Trader

Evenings we sat in his kitchen. "Italian TV disgusts!" he'd say, surfing. Eager contestants leaned their cleavage close to the screen for us. *The Beverly Hillbillies* sounded like dummies dubbed in Italian.

All the while he replayed his life for us: Uncle the clever merchant, hauling a load of firewood for his own profit, along with *Nonno Cecco's* milled deliveries. Uncle the trickster, siphoning power off the electric meter lords. Uncle the lover, marrying a young aunt when her reputation paled. "I'm telling you how it was," he'd say, his left hand open palm up, his right hand coming down on the left palm like a knife blade. "This is the truth!" he'd say, as if his insistence made the words history.

And he knew horses.

I translated for my wife, while blue light from the TV flickered off dark walls—Uncle Ivo was saving on electricity.

He replayed his part as an Italian on the Russian front where the Nazis wanted no wounded survivors. It had to be done, "Like this! Like this!" he said, pointing index finger and thumb, like a gun, as they do at the heads of lame horses.

And I'm thinking, now—as they do to those who have done the job, trying to survive, and I'm thinking, *Isn't the world a little better without some bad?*

And I'm thinking how all this is us, too, while I sit on this pier above a gentle lake where even the great blue heron, passing within range this morning, has an Uncle's old, old face.

Three:
In America

Covenant

In the harbor in Naples what would have happened if *Papà* and I coming back from a pilgrimage to the Church of the Assumption hadn't slipped past the guards and onto *The Saturnia* where *Mamma* waited waving our passports, the whole ship anxious to leave? Already having sounded the final horn? Already the tow ropes tightening?

What would have happened?

Mamma, desperate, would stand at the railing and look back and once out to sea but long, long after dark, would go below to her cabin in third class, to cry. In America she would make her own way, maybe getting a job, years before she did.

Seeing the big ship disappear, *Papà*, pale-white and trembling, would grab my hand and lead us from that low, dangerous place. Uncle Priest would fetch and take us back. In our mountain village we would wait again—the long wait. And since the war was over, eventually, we would be reunited—*Papà* and I with *Mamma* and little brother.

But in that desperate moment on the docks of Naples when we almost lost America and tasted a poor soul's fears as all you've managed to salvage sinks or floats away, I want to say that we were marked forever by the bitter and blessed.

"Be-Bop-A-Lula"

Gene Vincent and The Blue Caps are on the radio, so I do a little twist and take *Nonna* Carola by the hand. She's come to America on a visit with her son, Uncle Priest, *Don* Remo. "*Vieni, vieni,*"—Come, come, I say in Italian. I try to twirl her in a rock-and-roll spin, but she pushes at me.

"Leave me . . . Leave me be," she says. "You make me dizzy."

I move in close, singing, "Be-Bop-A-Lula," with the music, as I've practiced it for the eighth grade Talent Night. *Nonna* seems so much smaller than I remember. "I can look down on you now," I say, jostling her around a little to the music.

"Leave me . . . Leave me be," she says.

"Be-Bop-A-Lula," I sing in her left ear.

"Go on. Go on," she says pushing at me. "I'm still enough your *Nonna*"—Grandma. She pushes at me and raises a hand, as if to hit me as I remember. "Let me be. Let me sit and let's have a proper visit," *Nonna* Carola says, "if you want me to stay for supper."

Once, My Father Must Have Said,
"Adamo, He *Hava Nica Daughta—Italiana*"

Maybe I was there because sometimes I mowed for him. We
were standing at the side of his backyard on Second Street. My
1950 two-door, two-tone blue Buick, straight eight, was parked
so we could both see it as we talked.

That shine. A couple months later I would crease the length
of the rocker panel on the driver's side, when it scraped against
the concrete stand of a light post because I whipped the steering
wheel a little to the right and floored the pedal while backing
out of too tight a spot at Colonial—a man who'd come in the
ice cream parlor after me got served while I'd been standing
front and center waiting.

"You should take her for ice cream, one time . . . See," Adam
was saying. "She's a good one, my Tony, once you get to know
her. Here." He held out a folded ten-dollar bill. "Don't say I
talked to you. Give a call once, now you got a nice car. I'd ap-
preciate it. She'd make a good wife, my Tony. How old are you
now?" Adamo said.

I pushed the back of my hand gently against his holding the
folded ten dollars.

"Guys come around. Most I don't care for," he said. "You
seem a good *Paesan'*. Don't say nothin'." He nodded toward his
back door.

I saw Antonia coming out. She wore a blue, blue dress, and
she was smiling.

Aunt Gloria, Fare-thee-well

Everybody has an Aunt Gloria, a little too loud and opin-
ionated, whose dishes blend too much American to please the
buds of all who are related. One thing was certain, she didn't
can her own tomato sauce. She used ketchup and *Contadina*.
There was a loss in flavor. Her sauces too sweet and too red.
There was the divorce everyone held over her head.

When she died, she died done with her husband's family.
Uncle Jimmy went without last rites, and Aunt Gloria said she
had already heard her brother-in-law's homily.

Ivo of the Hammer

From the time of his arrival back in 1953, until he retired to a custom-built house in Altopascio, a home with American comforts like central heating, living room carpeting, and window screens, Uncle Ivo worked at Moline Malleable Iron Works, in "Belgium Town," in the Fox River valley. He worked at Moline for twenty-five years. Never missed a day—sometimes a dozen aspirins inside, against rheumatic pains. And if you didn't shaft him into some shit job, you could count on him for more work per hour than most men did.

While he lived in his red brick bungalow on Anderson Boulevard and we visited, he would talk about Moline and, with twinkling eyes and waving hands, he would expand on the ten-thousand springs and sprockets, hammer heads and chains he'd checked and sacked the weeks past.

And all this talking about hammers would remind him . . . as it now reminds me of Uncle Ivo's stories.

When we visited him in Altopascio, many a late night we sat in the dim basement kitchen, the blue screen of the TV flickering around the room and over us. He told stories he wanted me to write. Uncle Ivo, the five-foot-four local Ruota fascist, who kicked the butt of the six-foot party boss over words. Ivo the lover who felt sorry about the gossip and married Aunt Albertina. Ivo the Italian soldier forced to walk with Nazis on the Eastern Front, unwillingly killing wounded Russians and getting rheumatism in his lower back.

In that sequence, when Ivo the soldier came back on leave to Italy, he found an Italian dentist to pull fourteen teeth. He had heard that missing fourteen teeth would keep him from being sent back to the front. Mouth bleeding, he was thrown in the brig. "But what could they do?" Uncle Ivo said. "Good or bad, teeth gone. *Dentista* say *nothinga*. If go back *Rusia*, I die," he said.

Such are the tales that made "Ivo of the Hammer" a Thor of a man. His name got linked with hammers at Moline. The story goes that some hillbilly punk wanted to know the meaning of "*Dago*." Ivo told him, "No good *thinga*, this call to Italian man."

That fellow joked him. One day took the hammer Uncle needed for his work. Ivo went and retrieved it, and as he walked away, the guy called out, "*Dago!*"

Fire in his eyes, Ivo spun around and whipped that hammer like a battle axe. He said, "Next *tima* I *killa* you!"

The guy ducked. Next day he never showed.

The boss came round. The union shop-man passed by.

The boss said, "This must be 'Ivo of the Hammer,'" but nothing more, and then he walked away.

The hillbilly never did return. Everybody said that, anyway, he hadn't been there long and that he missed a lot of days.

Holiday Dinner

After the nuts, the green *torta* and chocolate *torta*, the *biscotti* and coffee, we laughed and laughed.

Aunt Maria *Nuova's* neck flared to her face with laughing. Her eyes watered. Her laughs bobbed her belly and her breasts along the table's edge, sending tremors and awakening the unbroken half-walnut shells I'd salvaged from the rubbish piles the adults had made and I had lined up like an armada on the white tablecloth sea.

Betrothal

It's Easter Sunday, and we have arrived in Chicago, at Aunt Maria's and Uncle Gino's, *Mamma's* brother, the Lenten bells all untied, my family gathered traditionally with *Mamma's* family, though her oldest brother, Uncle Jimmy, hasn't come, as usual. He's married to a divorcée with two daughters, and Aunt Gloria has never felt accepted, so they never come. *Mamma's* youngest sister Lilia is there with her husband and two daughters, the oldest, now with her husband Sal, who had come from Italy and been a boarder at Uncle Gino's.

I have come with my fiancé, a Protestant. We're not staying for dinner, and I have brought a bottle of pink champagne.

The gathering seems cordial, but the room feels unsettled, as if the usual clamorous talk and loud sprinkles of laughter before the meal have suddenly stopped, the last words snatched back out of the air, as when you walk to the window and make all the chattering birds at the feeder suddenly disappear. *Mamma* sits at the end of the couch, her face and mouth closed and drawn down like the Greek tragedy mask. Even the kitchen at the far end of the long hallway seems to have grown silent. Some of the women have come to stand in this dark hallway that ends at the dining room door.

I announce "Her," and at the extended rectangular table, not yet set but already covered with two white linen tablecloths end to end, I uncork the pink champagne, as someone questions the idea of a toast on empty stomachs. The first glass I pour bubbles over the sides, staining one of the tablecloths.

A Dead Horse

"My husband's dead. My husband's dead," she said and hung up.

Though *Mamma* knew the voice, she had to guess because Aunt Elena had always talked of her own husband as "Egisto."

When *Mamma* and *Papà* arrived, Aunt sat on the couch and said, "*Ohimena!*"—Oh dear me! She had already called most everyone, including Cousin Duilio in Rome. When Duilio said, "*Pronto,*" she said, "My husband's dead." He heard Aunt's voice and cried and couldn't say another word. "My husband's dead," Aunt Elena said again, and thinking of the charge, hung up.

Now she sat on the couch and said, "*Ohimena!*"—Oh dear me! *Mamma* and *Papà* sat, watching her hold one cheek in her hand, from eight to one, and Uncle Jerry lay dead on his bed.

The ambulance finally came out from Chicago, where Uncle had bought a couple first class drawers in the Mount Carmel Celestial Mausoleum, but the coroner held things up when they couldn't find Uncle's wallet. He kept it in his pants, but they couldn't find where he'd left his pants, and they couldn't ask him, and the coroner said Uncle couldn't be dead without proper ID, and without the wallet there was no telling who he was.

"*Ohimena! Ohimena!*" Aunt said. *Papà* walked up and down the hall, looking and went into Uncle's room to ask his older brother where he'd left his pants.

Aunt remembered his habit of hanging them on the vacuum cleaner handle, and she said, "*Ohimena. Ohimena,*"—Oh dear me! Oh dear me! like *Mamma* said it to us now.

Then *Papà* said, "Uncle Egisto was *un' deada cavallo*"—a dead horse. Four of us couldn't lift him off the bed. We let his feet and legs drop, dragged him to the kitchen where we rolled him on the stretcher. *Un' deada cavallo,*" he said and held one cheek in his hand.

What I Said at Aunt Albertina's Wake

The truth is Italian men did the posturing. They found the time and the space for it. They aged into characters. Their women stayed where they were, quiet at the back of a room. They wore grays, browns, and navy blues.

I think now of the almond paleness of their skin, the hands and cheeks you pressed in greetings and farewells—soft as peony petals. *Bricchi's* Carola, who stayed at home or sat at the back of a room so silent, you forgot she was there. Uncle Jerry's Elena, who cast a Democratic vote against his Republican one, but never said so and almost wrecked the car when Uncle Jerry tried once to teach her to drive. Their friend Emma, one of the few bold enough to drive, who always gripped the wheel with two hands and turned corners with two hands guiding the wheel as if she was running a hem under a sewing machine for a coat from the coat factory where she and *Mamma* and Aunt Albertina and a few other Italian women worked.

But mostly, when I think of this one, I think of how with her mouth she wet the folded corner of a tissue then dabbed at her eyes.

"So . . . Nephew, my dear nephew," she'd say to me, smiling, dabbing at her eyes, "we work up courage . . . I'm not made of hardness like your Uncle Ivo."

Remember those days when we were young and wore those Orlon scarves tucked in around our necks and upturned coat collars for warmth? That's how I remember these Italian women.

Breath of the Onion

He had been to America twice, maybe three times, the last time alone for a dozen years—and at least up until 1931. In the Great Depression that came, he was laid off from sulfur-tipping matches on *the line* of a factory above Niagara Falls.

Maybe that's where Alessandro was nicknamed *Favilla*—"Spark." He carried that name and what money he'd saved back to Ruota, where he bought a vineyard and a small olive grove and lived content. I knew him as *Nonno Favilla* and knew him by his onion breath because he loved onions and always needed a kiss before letting me listen to the *"ta-ta-ting, ta-ta-twang"* of his big pocket watch.

Nonno Favilla talked of having been to America, the long, hard voyages on ships, and never needed to go back.

The Fig Tree

"You pull down," he said, speaking Italian, his face red from the wind, his eyes watery. He slid the coil of rope up the four-inch trunk. He handed me the two rope ends and walked to the back side of the tree from me, between the tree and the broad side of the garage, and put his shoulder to the trunk.

I stepped toward the tree, my back to him and to the tree in front of him. I straddled the trench he had dug and pulled taut the rope ends I held, one in each hand.

"Don't fall in the trench and get buried yourself under the tree." He chuckled.

"*Tanti fichi*"—many figs. "Too *bada*," I said, "Why *rusha*?" I tried to say as much as I could in Italian, too, though often found myself forced to Italianize American words for which I didn't know the Italian equivalent. In Italy I had only attended school to the third grade.

"It's half November. North Illinois," he said. "*Pulla!* As much as you can! Where your *strengtha*? You need eat more *meata* and *drinka vino*."

Straddling the trench, I set and firmed both feet, wound the ends of the ropes, one around each wrist, and sliding the ropes over my shoulders like wagon shaves, I thought of the mule we once had in Ruota.

"At your age," he said, "I could . . ."

Straddling the seven foot ditch, I planted my feet like a loaded beast, bent my knees, and gave a heave. The tree lurched, pivoting forward on its half-loosened ball of dirt and half-cut roots. A crack echoed out of the trench and up the trunk.

"Woooo! Woooo!" my father said. "*Enougha* today. We do little more tomorrow." He came around, took the rope ends from me and tied them to stakes he'd driven beforehand in the ground, one along each edge of the trench.

Loose dirt slid in the trench as I lifted my left foot and righted myself on the right side of the bent-down fig tree. "We're leaving . . . Going home tonight," I said.

"What the hurry? Always hurry. Hurry. Doctor visits," he said. "Tomorrow Sunday."

"I have to get ready to teach, Monday."

"Always hurry. Always busy," he said. "Too busy."

I said, "You sure we can't finish *la joba* now?" I walked around to the back side of the tree and leaned forward, my shoulder onto the tilting trunk.

"No. No!" He came alongside and pushed at my shoulder. "Change *taka* time," *Papà* said.

I nodded and stepped back.

Spectral Bird

In the farm field of sculpted snow, the snowy owl is my grandmother, dead all these years, and I have come to visit.

Crusted snow or parched field in late summer, Nonna Nunziata is in the Tuscan sun on her patio below the garden. They haven't eaten and will want me to stay even without asking. Afterwards we'll talk about America, and she'll say all she wanted was to come home. Pregnant a third time and mostly sick, she thought she would die giving birth if she didn't come home. I'm sad and don't want to leave her.

A snowy owl in a winter afternoon goes through me—feathers ruffled and fluffed into bounds and curves of the grasses, drifted snow mounded and molded around us, swirled distant and out of our sight, the owl's yellow eyes, looking over our right shoulder.

Making Wine In the Midwest

I.

On a Saturday or Sunday in early October we would rise in the dark and in a car minus the back seat head for Chicago and the tracks along South Halsted Street where chocolatey wafts from the Hershey plant sweetened the air. Then in front of open train cars and stacks of boxes of California grapes sticky with juice, the coy vendors waved us in. They held up a cluster like a big-chested woman's jewels. At each stand, the taste of one grape was all you got. It had to do, and *Papà* would bargain and decide.

II.

Mamma said, "As those your *Papà's* age die off . . . for the young who are left it's a bother."

And every year the grapes brought in seemed fewer. Only two locations were left in Chicago: Twenty-Seventh Street at South Ashland and the tracks on Chicago Avenue. The Savoy Grocery was there, then. Fragrances filled your nostrils. Stacked in open crates along the floor were flat, salt-dried cods and halibuts, wheels of Milwaukee Stella cheeses—Romanos and Parmesans. Salamis, mortadellas, flank prosciutto hams, and pork blood sausages hung from the ceiling. And cluttering the space in front of the counters were open barrels (two deep) of dried pinto beans, of egg noodles, and open barrels of dried black olives in olive oil seasoned with garlic and parsley. The high-ceilinged, long, narrow space of Savoy enfolded and lifted you with fragrances. Even after half a lifetime, one wrinkly black olive or one waft of olive oil can bring you back.

The grape names on Chicago Avenue enchanted: *Zinfandel*, *Zibibbo*, *Colombana*, and *Moscato*. *Zinfandel* and *Colombana* were for red wine. *Zibibbo* and *Moscato* were for white (though *Papà's* white wine had a coppery tint from the yellow grapes). And there were Concords.

Names were turning American. Grapevines were becoming cold weather hardy and heading into prairie backyards.

III.

Papà planted Concord grapevines along the side of his garden, between his yard and the neighbor's and along the back fence. They grew, and then there were Concord grapes, red and pink and white, some years an abundance of grapes, and *Papà* made Concord grape wine, in spite of the daily visits to the not-quite-ripe fruit from squirrels and the nightly visits from raccoons. And he was thrifty. After he had drawn the wine off the sediment, he pressed the residue of skins and clusters in a small apple press. This wine was a *Second*. At lunches he drank it mixed with a little water.

IV.

Mamma complained each year as his garden crept a little farther into the backyard, but he recycled the pressed-out grape pulp into the soil, making his garden drunk with the smell and black and rich with the pulp's richness. If you said anything, he'd say it was a toast to his garden. He'd remind you about the flavor of even late-September tomatoes.

Then early each spring he would begin again by pruning his vines.

On a Road

Among the Eau Claire lakes where an unnamed sand road curved past a tamarack marsh and climbed a hill to a blacktop, Grandfather's image rose up to meet me. Whether an odor of marsh and trees and sand whisked the humid day into a waft of asphalt or an adult desire hounded a childhood memory beyond reason, *Nonno Favilla* rose up in a roomful of light.

Then it was easy to think how a hand stretched lovingly across might lead him willingly out of that place to this, for a little while. I know earth things shine back to the universe. A grandfather's earthshine must be there, traveling among starlight and always arriving, like the light of a long dead star . . . Still arriving.

And when I arrived even after forty years to that vineyard below the pines that crested the ridge, I could tell that new hands had layered the line fences. But down forty years of stones were the boulders *Nonno* picked up off his terraced rows and placed in those walls. As I sat in the early dawn, the humid Mediterranean haze pressed down the hollows and valleys below. I heard a cuckoo bird calling as I knew and remembered, calling toward the waking town, and I rose to meet whoever might come that way to work, someone else's grandfather, sure, but mine, too, for he'd passed that way.

Easter Visit

"Come out. Come out, Father!" I wanted to say. "Something's in the air." Instead I said, "It's a nice day," as we shuffled around half the block and to the back alley and stopped by the garage.

While he rested, I gave half a dozen pulls to the discarded rototiller he'd picked up off somebody's curb and had been tinkering with. He kept reaching to prime and nudge the engine that wouldn't start.

But by then I'd convinced his old legs, and we did the other half-block, out the alley and back to the front of his house, maybe now with a little spring in his step. His face reddened and shined in the setting sun.

I thought, *Live, Father. Live because you're alive. Live as long as you breathe.* I said, "Since you've surpassed the record of the oldest in your family, why not keep going?" And I said, "Drink water. Eat a banana . . . Why not walk a little every day?" I said, as if eighty-seven years were a drop and my words meant resurrection.

Coraggio e Avanti

The way he stood, talking to my dead father, you would have said Uncle Ivo was giving him advice on how to visit the Old Country.

And *Papà* would have listened, although Uncle wasn't telling him how to watch out for pickpockets in Genoa where on that first visit back *Papà* had his wallet lifted.

"*Fatti coraggio*, Fabio"—have courage, Uncle was saying, as if trying to encourage himself, too. "There's no turning back now that you've started. Soon you'll be there. It's better this way," Uncle was saying. "More for you than for us. Life is no life when you can't eat or drink a glass of wine. You know that, Fabio. So make the best of it. What else can we do? *Coraggio e Avanti*"—courage and forward.

I had followed Uncle Ivo up to the casket but stopped a little distance behind him, and as he turned toward me, he said, "*Si va là, là,*"—we plug along. He smiled. A touch of watery pink fringed the edges of his blue, blue eyes.

Mother, Your Father Is Missing From the Portrait

In the family portrait your father is missing from, you are beautiful. A smile set, perhaps, by the photographer, escapes the edges of your face and eyes darkly large and soft. Your own mother's finely lined face is hard-set, her hair already gray. Grandfather stayed in America too long that third time. Grandmother's eyes are thin slits. She grows distant in the picture. But you, you still warm out of your face—lovely, lovable girl.

You are photographed closest to your mother, and your father is missing from the portrait. Grandmother is a strong, distant woman, and your pushover father is missing from the picture.

Mamma's (*Torta Verde*) Green Pie Recipe

1. Mix a biscotti dough: $1/3$ cup butter, softened; $2/3$ cup sugar; 2 t baking powder; 1 t vanilla; 2 eggs; 2 cups flour; 1 T rum.

Roll out for pie crust and shape into pie pan. If dough is too sticky, dust with flour as you roll it out. Don't forget to make points, like a crown along the edge or lip of the pie pan.

2. Filling
$3/4$ c rice
$3/4$ c sugar
$1/4$ c raisins
$1/8$ c pine nuts or pecan pieces
2 eggs
a good handful of spinach or Swiss chard, chopped
dash of cinnamon
dash of nutmeg
dash of rum

3. Cook rice (you may want half water and half milk and a pat of butter, for creamier rice). Put cooked rice in a bowl and mix in finely chopped spinach or chard, plus all other ingredients. Put mixture in shell. Do a lattice top over the mixture. Bake at 350°, 45 min. to 1 hour.

Juice

He's had a urinary tract infection for months, he tells me and looks hounded and diminished, his five-foot stocky stance pale and joyless. He's back in America now, living near his daughter. The afternoon light from the living room windows catches his eyes, and I see the shine of cataract surgery implants, but I know his sight is focused inward, now, on his ailment.

"Cranberry juice. It works for that," I say, speaking Italian, and suddenly we're up and I'm taking him to the store as if he is the young visitor and I'm trying to entertain him, though he's Uncle Ivo, the Uncle Ivo who always took charge and directed when you traveled together, even if you drove your own car.

He has gotten old.

He buys ten cans and seems distracted in the supermarket, which I assume he has often frequented. On the way back home, he gets lost, though it's his town and the road to the market we came on. He says I'm going the wrong way and wants me to turn around. The desperate, spooked look of his eyes, the lines on his face begin to confuse me. I look around, trying to remember. I try to reassure him we're not lost.

Empty wine bottles and an empty wine jug are all he can find in the cupboards, so I try to think fast. Then I ask for an empty Mason quart jar he would have from tomato sauce. He only lets me add one can of cold water to the quart jar, believing the more concentration of juice, the speedier the cure. He fills a three-ounce glass, the type of small glass he and my father used to sample a newly drawn wine, and holds the glass up to the light, then tastes the liquid.

"Not *bada*," he says, rolling and spreading the juice on his tongue like a wine. He raises the glass to the light again. "*Chiaro*"—clear. He takes another swallow. "*Bel piccante*,"— Nice tang. "*Se lavora, e una buona medicina*,"—If it works, it's a good medicine. "*Una semplice cura*."— A simple cure. "*Tutti quei dottori e professori*,"All those doctors and professors. He waves his free hand through the air, dismissing them all. "*Te vieni. Mi porti una cura*,"—You come bring me a cure. "*Chi va mandato?*"—Who sent you to me?

From the door, he says, "Don't worry. I'll take the cure."

Feeling good for having visited and hoping the cure works, I whisper a prayer, *sotto voce*, as we drive away.

Grandfather Francesco

In the photograph he is standing by the mortared wall of washout stones, above a ravine. Flour dust from his mill is on the tops of his leather work boots and on the right knee of his pants, a sack of stone ground flour on his left shoulder, his wide brimmed hat tilted back and to the right, as if he has just climbed a mountain. Only his long face and white, droopy mustache are serious and aged, belonging to the *Nonno Cecco* I knew . . .

That *Nonno Cecco* is sitting by the fire in the left corner of the old kitchen, the kitchen of his house, where *Papà* brought his wife to live. *Nonna* Carola, *Nonno Cecco's* wife, is now living at the rectory of her youngest son, Uncle Remo, the priest. Having sent the young, unmarried Cousin Maria back home, *Nonna* Carola is Uncle Remo's housekeeper. So there, in *Nonno Cecco's* kitchen where we are, *Mamma* has a cabbage and bean soup steaming on the woodstove across the room from *Nonno Cecco*. Without using his cane he has shuffled over twice, to taste the boiling mixture and each time season it with a heavy layer of black pepper.

I'm saying how I saw our local priest's housekeeper dump a chamber pot out the second story window, onto *Via* Ruota, the main street. "Almost on top of me as I passed," I say.

"Don't be gossiping," *Mamma* says.

"You can't be certain," *Nonno Cecco* says. "Maybe it was holy water. She's an old one, that one. Have I told you about the old priest who kept a young housekeeper busy day and . . ."

"Go find *Papà*," *Mamma* says. "Supper is ready."

Nonno Favilla's Heirloom

Let the scent of onion cross the air, and you walk out of my mind, a green bunch in your hand. We enter your kitchen. Cabbage and bean soup steams in the soup plates. A bite of onion, a spoonful of soup heavy with bread, and you work up a sweat on your face. My mouth begins to burn. My eyes water. My nose starts to run, the room reeling with the odor of onion.

All the years melt away from my belt. I am sitting, a boy on your lap, a man in the head. For a kiss you let me listen to the sweet tick, echoing around the chamber of your watch. For two I'll pick you a bunch of my onions.

Acknowledgements

The author wishes to thank the editors of *Journal for the Study of Peace and Conflict*, *New Ohio Review*, and *The Thunderbird Review*, in which some of these anecdotes first appeared.

A small group of anecdotes was published in *Letters Not Sent*, a handmade, limited edition book from Robinson Lake Imprints.